JACK
and the
Animals

AN APPALACHIAN FOLKTALE

DONALD DAVIS

Illustrated by **KITTY HARVILL**

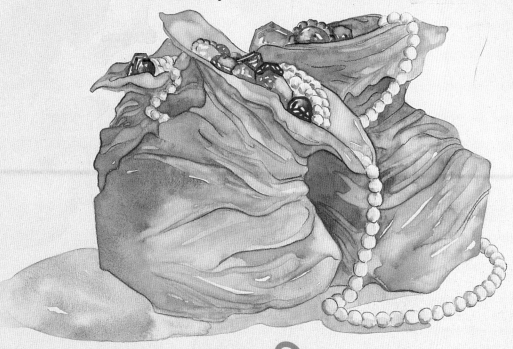

AUGUST HOUSE
Littlefolk

Published 1995 by August House LittleFolk,
P.O. Box 3223, Little Rock, Arkansas 72203,
501-372-5450.

Book design by Harvill Ross Studios Ltd., Little Rock
Manufactured in Korea

10 9 8 7 6 5 4 3 2 1   PB

LIBRARY OF CONGRESS CATALOGING-IN-PUBLICATION DATA

Davis, Donald D., 1944–
Jack and the animals / Donald Davis; illustrations by Kitty Harvill.
  p. cm.
Summary: An Appalachian version of the traditional tale in which a boy and five
elderly animals find their fortune in a robbers' den.
ISBN 0-87483-413-9 (hc)
ISBN 0-87483-620-4 (pbk)
[1. Folklore—Appalachian Region.] I. Harvill, Kitty, 1958– , ill. II. Title.
PZ8.1.D289Jaf   1995
398.2´097568´01—dc20
[E]   94-46966

First Hardcover Edition, 1995
First Paperback Edition, 2001

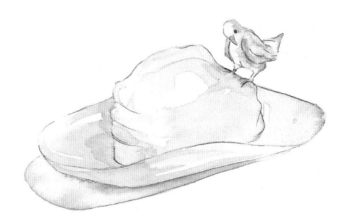

Grandmother lived in a big log house in the mountains. One day she finished her chores early and said to my cousins and me, "Let's go up on the mountain and cook our supper."

So we took a frying pan and eggs and bacon and walked back up above where the cows lived. There we gathered sticks, built a fire on a rock, and cooked our supper. When we had eaten, Grandmother told us a story about Jack.

One day Jack left home to seek his fortune. He didn't know that a fortune could be money or a job or even some adventures. He didn't know what a fortune was, but he was looking for it anyway.

While he was looking for his fortune, he passed a big barn.

From behind the barn he heard a terrible sound: *"Moo! . . . Moo-hoo! . . . Moo-hoo, hoo, hoo, hoo . . ."*

When he looked inside the barn, he was surprised to see a cow crying.

"Why are you crying?" Jack asked.

"I am so old I don't have any milk left," the cow answered.

"Then you should come with me to seek my fortune," Jack said.

And the cow came with Jack.

Passing by a house later, they heard another terrible sound:
"*Bow! . . . Bow-wow! . . . Bow-wow, oow, oow, oow . . .*"
When Jack looked toward the house, he saw a dog crying.
"Why are you crying?" Jack asked.
"I am so old I can't chase robbers," the dog answered.
"Then you should come with us to seek our fortune."
And the dog came with Jack and the cow.

As they were passing an apple orchard, they heard another terrible
sound: *"Mew! . . . Me-ow! . . . Me-ow, ow, ow, ow . . ."* It came from high up in
a tree, and when Jack looked, he saw a cat crying.

"Why are you crying?" Jack asked the cat.

"I am so old," the cat answered, "that I can't remember how to get down
out of the tree."

"Then you should come with us to seek our fortune," Jack said.

He helped the cat down from the tree, and the cat came with Jack and
the cow and the dog.

As Jack and his friends passed a hay field, they heard another terrible sound: *"Hee-haw! . . . Hee-haw! . . . Hee-haw, aw, aw, aw . . ."*

When Jack looked, he was surprised to see a donkey crying.

"Why are you crying?" Jack asked.

"I'm so old that I can't do any work," the donkey answered.

"Then you should come with us to seek our fortune," Jack said.

And so the donkey came with Jack and the cow and the dog and the cat.

The day was almost over, and still Jack and his friends heard another terrible sound: *"Cock-a-doodle-doo! . . . Cock-a-doodle-doo, oo, oo, oo . . ."*

The sound came from right on top of the barn they were passing, and when Jack looked up, he saw a rooster crying.

"Why are you crying?" Jack asked the rooster.

"I am so old that I can't tell if the sun is coming up or going down," the rooster answered.

"Then you should come with us to seek our fortune," Jack told the rooster.

And so the rooster came with Jack and the cow and the dog and the cat and the donkey.

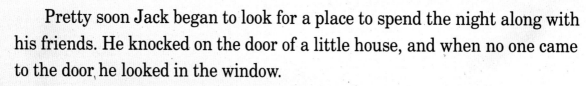

Pretty soon Jack began to look for a place to spend the night along with his friends. He knocked on the door of a little house, and when no one came to the door he looked in the window.

By candlelight he could see piles of gold and sacks of money and big bags of jewels. Jack thought, "This must be a robbers' hideout!" Then he saw a huge table covered with food.

Jack and his friends were just about starved, and they could see that whoever had started the meal had left in a hurry. So they decided to go inside and finish the meal.

Just as they finished eating, they heard footsteps on the porch. Jack was pretty sure it was the robbers coming home.

"Hide! Hide!" Jack told the animals.

While he blew out the candles, all of the animals hid.

The cat hid in the fireplace where the fire had gone out.

The dog hid behind the door.

The donkey hid behind a swing on the porch.

The cow hid in the bushes in the yard.

The rooster hid on top of the house, and Jack hid up in a tree.

One of the robbers came into the house to see why the candles were blown out while the other robbers waited in the woods. When the robber looked at the fireplace, he thought he saw coals glowing. He blew on them, hoping that the fire would blaze up. And when he did, he blew ashes right in the cat's eyes!

The cat screamed and came out of the fireplace, scratching the robber right in the face.

As the robber ran out the door, the dog came out and bit him all the way across the porch.

The donkey came out from behind the porch swing and kicked him off into the yard.

The cow caught him on her horns and tossed him out into the woods.

The rooster crowed, "Cock-a-doodle-doo! Cock-a-doodle-doo!" And Jack held onto the tree and tried not to fall out from laughing so hard!

The robber ran back to his friends, and they all ran far off into the woods before he told them what had happened.

"Our house is full of monsters!" he said. "There was a little one in the fireplace with terrible long claws. It tried to claw my eyes out.

"There was a medium-sized one behind the door with horrible long teeth.
It tried to eat me alive!

"A bigger one with at least five legs kicked me off the porch, then a huge one with horns tossed me in the woods. I got away from the worst one of all, though," he said.

"What could be worse than that?" the other robbers asked.

"There was a screaming monster on top of the house. It kept crying, 'Throw-him-up-here-too! Throw-him-up-here-too!' I don't know what it might have done to me. We can't ever go back."

The next day, Jack brought the sheriff to see the robbers' house. When the sheriff saw all that Jack had found, he said, "Jack, you have found a fortune!"

"So that's what a fortune is," said Jack.
And for getting rid of the robbers, the sheriff gave Jack and the animals the whole fortune to keep for themselves.

"And," Grandmother said, "since they had all that fortune to buy food with, Jack and his friends could be living there still."

ABOUT THE STORY

When I was a child in the North Carolina mountains, Jack was a little boy who was so familiar to me I thought he must live near my grandmother. Everytime I visited her house, she told me about Jack's latest adventures. By the time I was a teenager, I knew well several dozen stories about Jack, all from hearing them told by my grandmother or other local tellers.

In this oral tradition, stories were not stored in books but in memory. They came to life in active telling, to audiences who talked back and asked questions.

Jack came to the Appalachian Mountains in stories brought over the Atlantic from the British Isles, though he is to be found in other cultures under other names. The Jack I know lives in a world of Scots-Irish descent, a world of subsistence agriculture, a world that has not changed for generations and is just beginning to meet the world of twentieth century multi-cultured America.

This Appalachian version of "Jack and the Animals" is but one of many traditions featuring this story motif. In the Aarne-Thompson Type Index, this story belongs to Type 130, *The Animals in Night Quarters*. Children who read this book may note that they have heard a story like this before, probably in the Grimm Brothers' version from Germany, "The Bremen Town Musicians." When I

first met that version as a schoolboy, I reported to my mother that we read a story that was supposed to be about Jack but left him out! It also is found in Norwegian, Scottish, Irish, and English versions. This rich variety will help the young reader overcome the belief that any particular folktale is made of only one specific set of words.

This telling of "Jack and the Animals" is not an attempt to capture Jack in a particular set of words and pictures. Please tell the story in your own words, see Jack in your own imagination, and then you may help keep our oral tradition living and vibrant.

–D.D.